Lab Manual

to accompany

programming.java

An Introduction to Programming Using Java

Rick Decker
Stuart Hirshfield
Hamilton College

PWS PUBLISHING COMPANY

I(T)P *An International Thomson Publishing Company*

Boston • Albany • Bonn • Cincinnati • London • Madrid
Melbourne • Mexico City • New York • Paris
San Francisco • Singapore • Tokyo • Toronto • Washington

PWS PUBLISHING COMPANY
20 Park Plaza, Boston, MA 02116-4324

I(T)P ®
International Thomson Publishing
The trademark ITP is used under license.

Sponsoring Editor: *David Dietz*
Editorial Assistant: *Katie Schooling*
Technology Editor: *Leslie Bondaryk*
Marketing Manager: *Nathan Wilbur*
Production Manager: *Elise Kaiser*
Cover Designer: *Cyndy Patrick*
Manufacturing Buyer: *Andrew Christensen*
Text/Cover Printer: *Malloy Lithographing, Inc.*

Printed and bound in the United States of America.
98 99 00 01 — 10 9 8 7 6 5 4 3 2

ISBN: 0-534-95114-7

For more information, contact:
PWS Publishing Company
20 Park Plaza
Boston, MA 02116

International Thomson Publishing Europe
Berkshire House 168-173
High Holborn
London WC1V 7AA
England

Thomas Nelson Australia
102 Dodds Street
South Melbourne, 3205
Victoria, Australia

Nelson Canada
1120 Birchmont Road
Scarborough, Ontario
Canada M1K 5G4

International Thomson Publishing GmbH
Königswinterer Strasse 418
53227 Bonn, Germany

International Thomson Editores
Campos Eliseos 385, Piso 7
Col. Polanco
11560 Mexico D.F., Mexico

International Thomson Publishing Asia
221 Henderson Road
#05-10 Henderson Building
Singapore 0315

International Thomson Publishing Japan
Hirakawacho Kyowa Building, 31
2-2-1 Hirakawacho
Chiyoda-ku, Tokyo 102
Japan

Contents

Preface

Perhaps the two most significant insights that have emerged from computer science education in the past ten years are, first, that the object-oriented programming paradigm is an effective vehicle for introducing novices to a wide range of "programming in the large" issues, and, second, that directed, hands-on laboratory experience is the most effective means for conveying these issues to students. The Java programming language, with its object orientation and its platform-independent support for event-driven graphical-user-interface programming, provides a medium for exploiting the first of these insights. This laboratory manual and the accompanying textbook, *programming.java: An Introduction to Programming Using Java,* address the second. Through a series of engaging and realistic sample programs, each of which comes complete with a full set of program analysis, experimentation, coding, and testing exercises, this manual renders Java and the concepts of object-oriented programming accessible, tangible, and meaningful to students with no prior programming experience.

Each of the lab sessions begins with a brief description of the programming and Java language concepts to be addressed, and a listing of specific lab objectives. The exercises that follow typically begin with instructions to run one of the lab programs included on the disk found in the back of the manual (we call them "lablets," since they are Java applets), which provides the point of departure for subsequent exercises. (As a result, students spend less time typing, and more time programming.) Most of the exercises involve modifying, testing, and expanding a lablet in specific ways that require an understanding of the programming and language-specific concepts involved. Some of the exercises are more exploratory in that they encourage students to invent and/or perform a test that tells them something about Java. Finally, "Postlab Exercises," provided at the end of each lab, may require students to develop one of the lablets even further, or to apply the same principles demonstrated in the exercises to an altogether new problem. We use these Postlab Exercises as a source of homework assignments.

This manual does more, though, than provide sample programs and labora**t**
introductory programming course based on Java. It also imposes a**n**
Java-based topics that not only reflects our teaching experie**r**
plays directly to Java's object orientation. Specifically**,**
OOP from the top down. That is, we start by presentin**g**
OOP—classes, packages, and inheritance—and defer un**t**
quick introduction to the generic Java programming envi**r**
lab sessions are devoted to using and experimenting with **,**
(the "AWT"). Doing so allows us to provide students with **,**
to read and to use, all of which emphasizes basic OOP not**.**

tangible graphical output. [If you haven't seen Java before, you'll be impressed by how easy it is to write applets that produce very interesting graphical output using only straightline code (with no explicit control structures).] By the end of this section of the course (covering chapters 1 through 4), students are able to use the AWT to describe arbitrarily complex graphical user interfaces. More important, they are completely conversant in the basics of OOP and the use of Java packages.

The second group of labs (chapters 5 through 8) is devoted to implementing the behavior of some of the graphical objects that are generated in the earlier programs. For example, in the first part of the course students may develop programs that describe interfaces to a calculator, an elevator, a digital alarm clock, and the like. Then, in the second part of the course they add code behind these graphical shells to implement interesting and visually appealing applets that render the calculator functional, control the elevator, and wake up to the alarm.

This approach may seem backwards, or at least unconventional, to you. To be sure, the table of contents for this manual does not include chapters entitled "Selection Statements," "Loops," or even "Inheritance," or "Polymorphism." Rather, our chapter titles identify and explicate Java's strengths. By adopting a "classes first" OOP approach (which we feel is justified for many reasons, not the least of which is that an applets is a class), we encounter all of the "traditional" programming topics quite naturally in the context of using, describing, and implementing Java classes. For example, conditional statements are useful for responding to button events (in Chapter 5), loops are used to process collections of information (in Chapter 8), and I/O is presented in terms of processing keyboard and list events (Chapter 10). Other standard topics, like subprograms and parameters, inheritance, and polymorphism, are dealt with repeatedly and with increasing complexity in the context of using classes, beginning in Chapter 2. Java, by virtue of its language support for exceptions, threads, images, and sounds, even affords us opportunities to present a few "non-traditional" topics that are recognized as essential to training the programmers of tomorrow, which we do in lab sessions 9 through 12.

In adopting this lab-based, classes-first approach we make no explicit assumptions about how a course is organized. All that matters, in fact, is that the lab exercises get done during, before, or after (in our order of preference) covering the corresponding topics in class. Our experience indicates that students learn more during lab than they do listening to a lecture. So, we tend to lecture infrequently, and to rely heavily on these exercises. Each set of exercises (excluding the stlab Exercises) is designed to take from one to three hours of time "at the machine," nding upon the student's preparation and the amount of experimentation that they choose to

A Final Word about the Computer Environment

Before beginning the labs, a quick word is in order about programming environments. We have written many lab manuals, and have always had to make a critical decision before doing so. The issue was: Should we write the materials so that they are specific to a particular programming language implementation, programming environment, and computer, or write them so that they are as generic as possible? Having done it both ways, we know that neither is totally acceptable. Java, thank goodness, makes this (nearly) a moot point.

Because of its architecture neutrality, the lablets used in these exercises will work (with only minor differences in appearance) on any machine that has a Java interpreter. They can even be viewed from within any Java-compatible browser. To perform the exercises, you also need access to a "programming environment" that allows you to edit, save, and compile Java programs. This programming environment can be anything from a project-based IDE ("integrated development environment," like Roaster for the Macintosh, or Symantec Cafe for the PC) to a simple word processor and the JDK compiler. It is up to you in the exercises that follow to interpret the phrase "edit, compile, and run the program" so that it makes sense in your environment. Once you have done so, and have access to our lablets, you are ready to begin the first lab ... Enjoy!

That said, though, we should echo a disclaimer we make in the text. Java is sufficiently new that some development environments haven't quite caught up yet. Some aren't as "bulletproof" as they should be and some don't implement the language strictly according to the standard. While we've endeavored to test all the lablets on a number of different platforms, we wouldn't be surprised to find that, as they say, "your mileage might vary." For the time being, there's not much you or we can do about that but wait for things to improve. If you do find any inconsistencies, please don't hesitate to let us know—perhaps by the second edition we might be able to take this paragraph out.

Rick Decker
Stuart Hirshfield

CHAPTER 1

❦

Background

This set of lab exercises is somewhat different from those that will follow in at least three important ways. First of all, out of necessity it focuses on using your Java programming environment rather than on the Java language *per se*. We must get through these "system" preliminaries in order for you to begin developing your programming expertise in subsequent chapters. Second, whereas most labs will begin with running one of the sample lab programs (the "lablets") we have provided, in this case you don't yet know enough Java to make much sense of a program. Not to worry—we'll guide you through one so that you can make it work and understand its output. Finally, in most other labs you are provided with copies of the lablets that you will need for your lab exercises. Given that the primary purpose of this lab is to show you how to use your Java system to create working programs, you begin this lab on your own, by typing in your first Java program.

Lab Objectives

In this lab, you will:

❦ Become familiar with your Java programming environment.

❦ Learn how to enter, edit, run, and save Java programs.

❦ Gain experience fixing some simple syntax errors.

❦ Investigate a variety of Java applets that demonstrate how useful and widely applicable the language is.

Exercises

1. Java programs come in two basic flavors—"applications" that are written to be run as standalone programs, and "applets" which are written to be run from within Worldwide Web (WWW) pages. Since almost all of the programs that we will be working with in these labs are of the applet variety, we refer to them collectively as "lablets."

    In order to run a lablet, you must perform four steps. First, the Java source code for the lablet must be typed in and saved as a file. This can be accomplished using any word processing program, or by using any of the programs that provide integrated development environments (IDEs) for Java. The name of this source file must consist of the name of the "public class" defined in the file, followed by the extension ".java". So, for our lablet below in which we define the class Colors, we would save our file that contains the program text with the name "Colors.java".

    Once this source file has been created, the next step is to *compile* it—that is, translate it into the Java byte code that can be interpreted and run on your computer. This, too, can be accomplished in a number of ways, ranging from invoking the Java compiler (typically called "Javac") from a command line, to choosing the "compile" command in an IDE. Whichever compiler you are using, it will translate your ".java" file ("Colors.java" in this lab) and produce a second file called a class file (named, in our example, "Colors.class").

    Step three in the process involves creating an HTML file that references the class file that we want to run. Many of the project-based IDEs produce such a file for you automatically. You may, though, have to type (again, using any word processor) a few lines (like those shown below as "example1.html") to create this file "by hand."

    It is the HTML file that can be run (or, more precisely, interpreted and viewed) by any applet viewer or Java-enabled browser. Again, depending on your programming environment, this may entail running a browser and opening your HTML file, sending the HTML file to your applet viewer, or running a project in an IDE.

    Clearly, the details of how you accomplish these steps (creating the Java source file, compiling it to produce one or more class files, creating an HTML file that references the class file, and viewing the HTML file) depends entirely on the combination of tools you have available to you for creating and running Java programs. Your instructor will provide you with the information you need to use your tools to accomplish these steps. Once you have this information, and have access to a computer, you can perform the following tasks.

a. Type the contents of the source file "Colors.java" exactly as it appears, below. Beware that the Java compiler distinguishes between upper- and lower-case characters (and, thus, regards the term Colors as different from the term colors). So should you!

```java
// My First Applet
// Watch the colors change as you click the buttons

import java.awt.*;
import java.applet.*;

public class Colors extends Applet
{
    Font f = new Font("Helvetica",Font.BOLD,18);
    int colorOfBackground = 0;
    int colorOfText = 0;
    Button backButton,textButton;
    Dimension myAppletDim;

    public void init()
    {
        backButton = new Button("Background Color");
        add(backButton);

        textButton = new Button("Text Color");
        add(textButton);
    }

    public boolean action(Event e, Object o)
    {
        if(e.target == backButton)
            colorOfBackground = ++colorOfBackground % 4;
        if(e.target == textButton)
            colorOfText = ++colorOfText % 3;
        repaint();

        return true;
    }

    public void paint(Graphics g)
    {
        switch (colorOfBackground)
        {
            case 0: setBackground(Color.cyan); break;
            case 1: setBackground(Color.orange); break;
            case 2: setBackground(Color.red); break;
```

(continued)

```
            case 3: setBackground(Color.black); break;
            default: setBackground(Color.cyan); break;
        }

        switch (colorOfText)
        {
            case 0: g.setColor(Color.blue); break;
            case 1: g.setColor(Color.magenta); break;
            case 2: g.setColor(Color.green); break;
            default: g.setColor(Color.blue); break;
        }

        g.setFont(f);
        myAppletDim = size();
        g.drawString("Goodbye World! Hello Java!!",
                    (myAppletDim.width/2) - 120,
                    (myAppletDim.height/2) + 20);
    }
}
```

b. Save the file as "Colors.java".

c. Compile the file "Colors.java".

d. Correct any syntax errors detected by the Java compiler by editing the offending line or lines.

e. Repeat steps (c) and (d) until your file compiles successfully, producing the class file "Colors.class".

f. Run "Colors.class". This may require that you create an HTML file that refers to your class. If so, the HTML file named "example1.html" below will work.

```
<HTML> <HEAD> <TITLE>Colors</TITLE> </HEAD>
<BODY> <HR>
    <APPLET CODE = "Colors.class" WIDTH = 400 HEIGHT = 200>
    </APPLET> <HR>
    <A HREF = "Colors.java">The source.</A>
</BODY>
</HTML>
```

g. Make sure that the window in which your applet is running is large enough to see the text that it displays. This may involve changing the values of the "width" and "height" parameters in the HTML file created by your IDE to match those above, or it may simply involve manually resizing the window in which the applet is being viewed.

2. Even though you might not have seen a Java program "in person" before, you can probably guess how this lablet accomplishes what it does by reading the source code. Look at the file "Colors.java" and notice its first couple of lines. They begin with the characters "//", which signal to the compiler that these lines serve as comments. That is, they aren't Java statements and are ignored by the compiler in translating your program. They are there strictly for the reader.

Comments can be added almost anywhere in a source file to explain what the code is trying to accomplish, or how it is doing what it is doing. In fact, comments can contain any text you want to include in your Java file.

a. Add some comment lines to your copy of "Colors.java" now that describe how you think the program is working.

b. Compile and run the commented version of the program to make sure it runs as did the original.

3. For all subsequent chapters, every lab will contain exercises that ask you to extend lablets to describe some additional information or to perform some additional processing. Usually, these exercises require that you do some programming on your own. Clearly, we're not quite ready for that here in Chapter 1, so we will provide you with the code needed to extend our first applet in a simple way. As with the original lablet, you may or may not understand the code itself—don't worry about that for now. Think of the following as exercises in using your Java environment to edit, compile, and run Java programs.

a. Edit the file "Colors.java" as follows. These changes will allow your program to display some additional colors. (If your environment allows cutting, copying, and pasting of text, these operations will come in handy here.)

i. Change the line in the `action` method that reads:
```
colorOfBackground = ++colorOfBackground % 4;
```

to read:
```
colorOfBackground = ++colorOfBackground % 5;
```

5

ii. Change the line that reads:
```
colorOfText = ++colorOfText % 3;
```

to read:
```
colorOfText = ++colorOfText % 5;
```

iii. In the paint method, after the line that reads:
```
case 3: setBackground(Color.black); break;
```

add the line:
```
case 4: setBackground(Color.white); break;
```

iv. After the line that reads:
```
case 2: g.setColor(Color.green); break;
```

add the lines:
```
case 3: g.setColor(Color.pink); break;
case 4: g.setColor(Color.yellow); break;
```

b. Compile and run your program to make sure that it performs as you expect, correcting any typos that you might have made along the way.

c. Change the line near the end of "Colors.java" that reads:
```
g.drawString("Goodbye World! Hello Java!!",
    (myAppletDim.width/2)-120,(myAppletDim.height/2)+20);
```

so that your name appears between the quotation marks, like:
```
g.drawString("Rick and Stu",
    (myAppletDim.width/2)-120,(myAppletDim.height/2)+ 20);
```

d. Compile and run your program until it correctly displays your name in the applet window.

4. Now it is time to explore some of the many applets that are available for viewing to anyone with an applet viewer or a Java-enabled Worldwide Web browser. If you have Web access, check out some of the following sites, and run the applets that they provide:

Yahoo's Main Java Page
```
www.yahoo.com/Computers_and_Internet/Programming_Languages/Java/Applets
```

Gamelan
www.gamelan.com/pages/Gamelan.html
The Java Boutique
www.j-g.com/java
JARS-Java Applet Rating Service
www.jars.com
Java Gallery
www.globalpresence.com/gal_java.htm

Postlab Exercises

1. Look through your text book and pick out any of the applets used as examples. Then, enter, edit, compile and run them.

CHAPTER 2

Applets

Now that you are basically familiar with your Java programming environment, we can shift our attention to understanding and using the Java language to describe and solve problems. That, after all, is the real focus of this course.

In this and all subsequent labs, the sample lablets are provided for you on disk so that you can begin the exercises immediately without having to type any lengthy programs. The Chapter 2 lablet is a class that uses a few of Java's built-in class libraries to identify and display some basic information about your programming environment. We will use it to investigate the basic structure and syntax of Java programs.

Lab Objectives

In this lab, you will:
- ❦ Compile many versions of the Chapter 2 lablet, *Snapshot,* to practice interpreting and fixing syntax errors.
- ❦ Run different versions of the lablet to see how changes to the program produce changes in behavior.
- ❦ Extend the lablet—on your own—to report additional system properties and to present the information in different formats.

Exercises

1. Before we set you off to do some programming of your own, we will walk you through this chapter's lablet pointing out many Java language features . Since we introduce a wide range of topics, we'll use a shotgun approach to analyzing the lablet.

   All of the items below describe editing tasks we want you to perform on the original version of the *Snapshot* lablet. For each editing task, your job is to describe the error that results (if one does) from the change we ask you to make to the lablet. That is, write down in the space provided the error message produced (if many error messages are produced, just record the first one), the offending linc(s) of the file, your guess as to the cause of the error, and whether the error was detected when compiling, or running your program. If no error was produced, indicate this and describe why the program still runs and how its behavior differs from that of the original lablet.

   You should proceed as follows: First, change the file "Snapshot.java" as described. Then, try compiling the edited version of the file. If it compiles successfully, run the program and note its behavior.

   Start out by saving a backup copy of the original version of "Snapshot.java". You should use it as the starting point for each editing exercise below. Note that when you are asked to "remove" a line from the file, the same effect can be achieved by simply inserting comment symbols ("//") at the start of that line. After each step, restore the applet to its original form.

   a. Remove the line that reads:
   ```
   import java.awt.*;
   ```

   b. Remove the line that reads:
   ```
   import java.util.Properties;
   ```

   c. Remove the word "public" from the line that reads:
   ```
   public class Snapshot extends Applet
   ```

   d. Remove the phrase "extends Applet" from the line that reads:
   ```
   public class Snapshot extends Applet
   ```

   e. Remove the line that reads:
   ```
   Font f1 = new Font("Times Roman",Font.ITALIC,18);
   ```

f. Remove the word "public" from the line that reads:
```
public void init()
```

g. Remove the line that reads:
```
resize(450,300);
```

h. Remove the "}" from the line following the line that reads:
```
resize(450,300);
```

i. Remove the phrase "Color." from the line that reads:
```
g.setColor(Color.black);
```

j. Remove the phrase "g." from the line that reads:
```
g.setColor(Color.white);
```

k. Remove the line that reads:
```
Date thisDay = new Date();
```

l. Move the line that reads:
```
Font f2 = new Font("Helvetica",Font.PLAIN,12);
```

from its current location to follow the line that reads:
```
Dimension myAppletDim = size();
```

m. Move the line that reads:
```
Font f2 = new Font("Helvetica",Font.PLAIN,12);
```

from its current location to follow the line that reads:
```
resize(450,300);
```

n. Move the line that reads:
```
Dimension myAppletDim = size();
```

from its current location to follow the line that reads:
```
Font f2 = new Font("Helvetica",Font.PLAIN,12);
```

o. Move the line that reads:
```
Dimension myAppletDim = size();
```

from its current location to follow the line that reads:
```
resize(450,300);
```

p. Change the line that reads:
```
public void paint(Graphics g)
```

to read:
```
private void paint(Graphics g)
```

q. Remove the phrase ".width" from the line that begins:
```
g.drawRect(15, 15, myAppletDim.width . . . ;
```

r. Move the entire body of method `paint` from its current location (leaving only the enclosing braces {}) to follow the line that reads:
```
resize(450,300);
```

2. Now, let's try to extend our lablet (starting, of course, with the original version of `Snapshot.java`) to perform some different operations. The first extension is just a simple change to reflect your taste in colors. Notice how throughout the `paint` method the current drawing color is changed (using method `g.setColor`) so that different parts of the screen appear in different colors..

   a. Change any or all of these to display the system information in whatever colors you see fit. By the way, the `Color` variables that appear in the original *Snapshot* (`black`, `white`, `lightGray`, etc.) are only some of those that are available directly from class `Color`. You can also make any graphic appear in `cyan`, `darkGray`, `green`, `orange`, `pink`, or `yellow`.

   b. You don't have to rely on predefined system colors to color your screen—you can mix your own by creating a new `Color` variable. For example, replace the line from the original `Shapshot.java` that reads:
```
g.setColor(Color.black);
```

   (where we are drawing the heading) with the following two lines:
```
Color myColor = new Color(200,20,100);
g.setColor(myColor);
```

   The first line will declare a new variable (`myColor`) and initialize it to a new object of type `Color`. This object, though, is not one of the predefined colors (like `blue` or `black`), but rather is created by mixing relative amounts of red (200, in this case), green (20), and blue (100). On our machines this produces a kind of reddish-purple, which is then used to display the heading on the screen.

Now, create some colors of your own and set different parts of the screen to display in these original colors.

3. Extend the lablet to report some other system properties, all of which are accessible from the `Property` class. You can, for example. determine the vendor of the Java implementation you are running (using `getProperty("java.vendor")`), the user name for the machine you are using (`"user.name"`), the Java class path for the current applet (`"java.class.path"`), and the operating system architecture (`"os.arch"`).

Revise `Snapshot.java` to report some or all of these properties. You will probably have to rearrange the positions of some of the strings drawn on the screen, and may even want to change the sizes of the fonts used.

4. To appreciate the need for the final extension we will propose, it helps to run the lablet (either the original, or any of the working extended versions that you have produced) again.

   a. Run the lablet. Once the snapshot report is displayed on the screen resize the applet window to a variety of shapes. Notice how the sizes of the snapshot rectangles that enclose the text adjust to reflect any window size. Looking at the code that paints these rectangles makes it clear why this happens. The locations at which these rectangles are drawn are recomputed each time the window is redrawn (which happens whenever we change the size of the applet window) using the current size of the applet window (as determined by the `size()` function and stored in `myAppletDim.width` and `myAppletDim.height`).

   b. The "Software Snapshot" heading, on the other hand, does not recenter itself as the size of the applet window changes. That is because it is drawn at a fixed location within the window. Change the program so that the heading is centered (or nearly so) no matter what the size of the applet window is.

Postlab Exercises

1. Write an applet that draws a digital clock or watch on the screen and displays the current time on its face. We're not asking you to write the program so that the time is continually updated (that will come later). For now, just display the time when the applet was started. You can use the `Date` class to retrieve the current time, as follows:

```
Date myTime = new Date();
int myHour = myTime.getHours();
int myMinute = myTime.getMinutes();
int mySecond = myTime.getSeconds();
```

2.   Write an applet that displays a page from an appointment book for the current date. We leave it to you to design the page any way you like. Check out the documentation describing built-in class Graphics, and you'll see that it provides methods for drawing a number of common shapes.

CHAPTER 3

Widgets

Gigobite, the lablet for this chapter, displays an order form that might be used in a modern fast food restaurant. You can select items to be ordered, indicate other features about the order, and then click on a button to "place the order." Since we haven't shown you how to write the Java code to get your applets to respond to the user's choices and instructions, our order form doesn't actually do anything with your order information. It does, though, demonstrate how easy it is to create and manipulate Java widgets to produce interactive, visually appealing, and interesting applets.

Lab Objectives

In this lab, you will:

❦ Run the Chapter 3 lablet, *Gigobite,* and make use of its widgets.

❦ Experiment with the lablet by changing the properties of its widgets, and observing the changes in the applet's appearance.

❦ Add some widgets of your own to extend the applet.

Exercises

1. The lablet for this chapter presents to you a collection of Java's widgets—the built-in buttons, lists, choice boxes, labels, text fields and text areas that are used to create

graphical user interfaces—for you to interact with. Your job at this point is to run the program and to see how its appearance is described in the Java source code.

a.   Compile and run the lablet now. Resize the applet window until the screen looks something like the figure below.

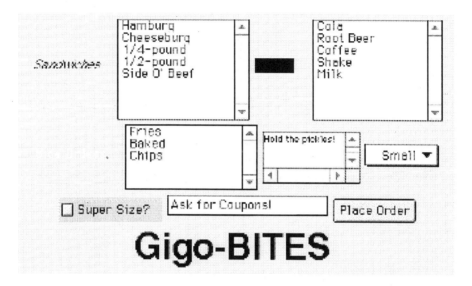

b.   Use the applet. That is, click on its list items, its check boxes, and its buttons. Enter some text in the text fields and areas.

c.   Part of the Java source code for the `Gigobite` class is listed below. The listing is annotated with questions (in bold face) about how the code describing the widgets relates to how the widgets are displayed. Answer the questions below by looking at the applet window, and by using any Java documentation that you have access to.

```
import java.awt.*;
import java.applet.*;

public class Gigobite extends Applet
{
    Checkbox superSize = new Checkbox("Super Size?");
```

What does 18 signify in the following line?
```
    TextField reminder = new TextField("Ask for Coupons!",18);
```

What is the difference between true and false in the following three lines?

```
List sandwiches = new List(5,true);
List drinks = new List(5, true);
List sides = new List(3, false);
Choice sizes = new Choice();
```

What do 2 and 10 mean in the following line?

```
TextArea comments=new TextArea("Hold the pickles!", 2, 10);
Button order = new Button("Place Order");
Label label1 = new Label("Sandwiches");
Label label2 = new Label("Drinks");
Label label3 = new Label("Side Orders");
Font myFont1 = new Font("Helvetica",Font.BOLD,36);
Font myFont2 = new Font("Helvetica",Font.ITALIC,12);

public void init()
{
    ...
}

public void paint(Graphics g)
{
    setBackground(Color.yellow);
```

What is the effect of the following statement?

```
g.setColor(Color.blue);
g.setFont(myFont1);
```

What font is used for the following drawstring instruction? What does 135,280 signify?

```
g.drawString("Gigo-BITES", 135, 280);
```

What does 90,100 signify in the following line?

```
sizes.resize(90,100);
```

What is the effect of the following statement?

```
label1.setFont(myFont2);
label2.setBackground(Color.cyan);
label3.setForeground(Color.white);
}
}
```

2. It is time to experiment a bit more actively with the class `Gigobite`. Here we'll ask you to change the program, re-compile it, and run it to observe differences in its appearance.

    a. First, alter the order in which the items are added to the sandwich list. Do the same for the `sizes` choice box. Compile and run your revised program, noting the differences you detect.

    b. Now, change the order in which the widgets themselves are added to the applet. Compile and run program and, again, note how your changes to the code are reflected in the applet's appearance.

    c. Notice how, in the `paint` method of the original code, the fonts, sizes, background and foreground colors of individual components can be specified. Write the code to change the sizes, font, and colors of any of the existing widgets. Compile and run your version of the applet to test it out.

3. We can now talk about making more extensive changes to class `Gigobite`. Use the original code as a model for making the following extensions. Compile and run the applet after each stage to make sure that it behaves as you expect it to.

    a. Add widgets to the `Gigobite` applet to describe a few different "Combo-Meals" (that is, combination meals composed of a sandwich, a side order, and a drink). Describe the combo-meals in a list, and add a label that identifies the list. Then, add a few combo-meals as items to your list.

    b. Follow the same basic procedure as in part (a) to add widgets to the *Gigobite* applet to describe a desserts menu.

    c. Add a check box to indicate that the current order is "Special"—that is, requires some special action.

    d. Add a choice widget that indicates whether a particular order is for eating in or taking out.

    e. Finally, add code to the lablet that draws some simple logo for *Gigobite* around or near the name on the applet window. The logo can be in the form of a text slogan, or can be some type of figure drawn using Java's basic drawing commands.

Postlab Exercises

1. Write an applet that displays an order form for some merchandise. You can use an order form that you have seen on the Worldwide Web as an example (look at the order form for downloading a new version of Netscape), or look in any mail-order catalog for a simple form to lay out on the screen.

CHAPTER 4

Visual Design

You saw in Chapter 3 how easy it is to use Java's built-in classes for describing widgets to build interesting looking (if not particularly functional) applets. You now can create and customize your own buttons, text containers, choice boxes, labels, and lists. You do not, though, have any direct means for grouping widgets together into a single, more complex component. Neither do you have a good way to control their placement on the screen. In this lab you will see how to address both of these problems.

Java provides us with a variety of container types, which can be used to hold and group widgets, as well as a few layout managers which help us to describe how the components and containers in our applet relate to one another spatially on the screen. Once you see how these containers and layout managers operate and how to take best advantage of them, you will be able to describe arbitrarily complicated interfaces in a consistent—and machine independent—way.

Lab Objectives

In this lab, you will:
- ❦ Run and experiment with this chapter's lablet, *Ovenator*.
- ❦ Practice using Java containers to arrange and rearrange the widgets that make up *Ovenator*.
- ❦ See the effects of using different layout managers on the appearance of the applet.
- ❦ Extend the *Ovenator* interface to add and position containers of your own.

Exercises

1. We will start this lab as we have started others, by running our lablet to see how it
    performs in its original state. Don't be concerned by *Ovenator's* lack of responsiveness.
    We haven't written the applet to do anything other than to look like a microwave oven.

    a. Compile and run *Ovenator* now. It should appear on your screen pretty much as it
        does in the following figure.

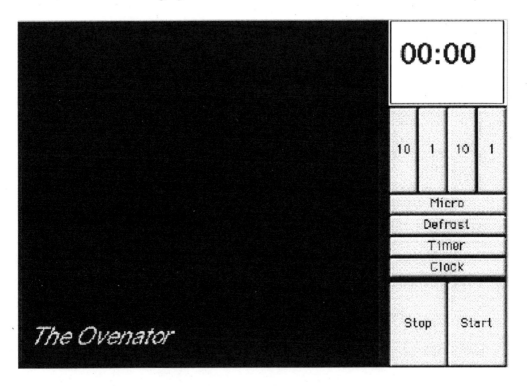

    b. Look at the code in "Ovenator.java" and identify the containers that were used to
        produce the microwave's interface. Then, on the figure above, draw a rectangle
        around each container and label it with the container's name and the Java layout
        manager that it uses. [Hint: There are 6 different containers, each with its own
        layout manager.]

2. Let's edit the source code to induce some simple errors—or, at least, changes—in how
    Ovenator uses its containers and layout managers. As we have done in previous labs,

make each of the following changes to the original lablet. Then, compile and run the edited version. In each case, explain the error that occurs or the difference in behavior that results from the change.

a.　Change the line in the `init` function that reads:
```
add("East", myControls);
```

to:
```
add(myControls);
```

b.　Remove (or just "comment out") from the `ControlPanel` constructor method the line that reads:
```
setLayout(new GridLayout(4,1));
```

c.　Change the line in the `TimeButtonsPanel` constructor method that reads:
```
setLayout(new GridLayout(1,4));
```

to:
```
setLayout(new GridLayout(2,2));
```

d.　Remove (or just comment out) the line in the `CookButtonsPanel` constructor method that reads:
```
bMicro = new Button("Micro");
```

e.　Remove (or just comment out) the line in the `CookButtonsPanel` constructor method that reads:
```
add(bTimer);
```

3.　Now let's make some changes to *Ovenator* that will affect the applet's appearance in more positive ways (that is, without introducing errors).

a.　First off, notice how by grouping widgets into containers (panels in our lablet), we can easily control the properties—like the color—of the containers as a whole. Change the colors of *Ovenator's* individual panels to suit your taste. Compile and run your revised applet.

b.　Notice the ordering of the Start and Stop buttons in the original lablet. Change *Ovenator* now so that these keys appear in the reverse order (that is, with "Start" to the left of "Stop"). Compile and run your revised applet.

    c.   Despite its sleek and stylish appearance, *Overnator* is missing something very important—a way to open its door. On many modern microwave ovens this is accomplished by means of a button that, when pushed, releases the door. Add a button to the control panel that would, in our virtual world, open the oven's door.

4. It is time to make some more significant extensions to *Ovenator*. Each of the following extensions will require that you add new components to the applet and position them on the screen. You can either add components to one of *Ovenator's* existing panels, or you can define new panels and add them to the applet directly. Feel free to rearrange any of the existing panels to accommodate your extensions.

    a.   Add four more "cooking" buttons to turn our oven into a combination convection/microwave. Name the buttons "Reheat", "Bake", "Broil", and "Combo".

    b.   Replace the current set of time-setting buttons (for 10 and 1, minutes and seconds) with a 12-key numeric keyboard. That is, the timer keys should include individual keys for 0 - 9, plus a button to set the minutes (labelled "MIN") and one to set the seconds ("SEC").

Postlab Exercises

1. Write an applet that displays a control panel for a graphing calculator. You can use a real calculator as a model, or make one up.

2. Do the same for an elevator control panel.

3. Do the same for a soda machine control panel.

CHAPTER 5

Java Language Basics

Up to this point, our lablets have produced user interfaces that look great on the screen, and even look like they might be easy to use. Unfortunately, we haven't been able to use them to do anything. That, of course, was due to the fact that we had not yet written Java code to produce and control the behavior of applets, other than those statements required to draw and place interface elements on the screen. In this chapter we will examine more closely the basic statements that are the building blocks of Java programs, many of which we have seen already, but haven't considered in any detail. We'll experiment with, for example, some of Java's built-in data types and operators, its String class, a variety of assignment and selection statements, and the issue of visibility (that is, what is declared as public, what is declared as private, and why) to discover why our lablets are written like they are.

The lablet for this chapter simulates a simple soda machine, and does so in behavior as well as appearance. You insert coins into the machine and select a brand by clicking buttons. The machine lets you know when it dispenses a drink, returns change (when asked to do so, by clicking the coin return), and even indicates when it is out of a certain brand. In short, this program uses Java statements to produce our first truly interactive program.

Lab Objectives

In this lab, you will:
- Run and experiment with the *SodaPop* lablet to see how it uses a variety of statements to produce realistic behavior.
- Modify *SodaPop* to introduce some errors related to the program's use of Java's built-in data types and its rules for visibility.

☙   Extend the soda machine's performance by modifying the program's existing methods, and adding new classes.

Exercises

1.   The *SodaPop* lablet should be pretty easy for you to use, assuming that you have used a soda machine before. The only difference between using our lablet and using the real thing (and it's a big difference if you're thirsty!) is that our's is a virtual machine. You insert coins by clicking on buttons. Drinks are dispensed by means of a message in a text field. You get the idea.

   a.   Compile and run *SodaPop* now. Use the applet to insert combinations of coins, buy many sodas, and return change. See what happens when you try to buy more than 5 colas.

   b.   Let's see now how the behavior of the program is reflected in its code. In the listing of "SodaPop.java" that follows, we have inserted "empty comments" (that is, comment indicators (//) that were intentionally left blank). Your job is to fill them in with comments describing the statement(s) that they are attached to.

```
import java.applet.*;
import java.awt.*;

public class SodaPop extends Applet
{
    . . .

    public void init()
    {
        . . .

        cost = 75;              //_____
        numberColas = 5;        //_____
    }


    public boolean action(Event e, Object o)
    {
        if (e.target == nickelButton)
```

```
    {
        processNickelButton();
        return true;          //_____
    }
    . . .
    else return false;        //_____
}

public void paint(Graphics g)
{
    . . .
}

private void processNickelButton()
{
    display.setText("Nickel inserted...");
    amount += 5;
}

private void processDimeButton()
{
    display.setText("Dime inserted...");
    amount += 10;        //_____
}

private void processQuarterButton()
{
    . . .
}

private void processReturnButton()
{
    String amountString;
    int dollars = amount / 100;  //_____
    int pennies = amount % 100;  //_____

    if (pennies < 10)      //_____
        amountString = new String("$" + dollars + ".0" + pennies);
    else
        amountString = new String("$" + dollars + "." + pennies);
    display.setText(amountString + " returned.");
    amount = 0;           //_____
}

private void processColaButton()
{
    if(amount >= cost)                                      (continued)
```

```
        {
            display.setText("COLA dispensed!!!");
            amount -= cost;
            numberColas--;      //_____
        }
        if(numberColas <= 0)
        {
            choices.colaButton.disable();   //_____
        }
    }

    private void processDietButton()
    {
        if(amount >= cost)          //_____
        {
            display.setText("DIET dispensed!!!");
            amount -= cost;
        }
    }

    . . .

}


//------------------------------------------------------------------


class ChoicePanel extends Panel
{
    public Button  colaButton,      //_____
                   dietButton,
                   liteButton,
                   rootButton;

    . . .

}
```

c. We'll modify *SodaPop* now to induce some common errors and simple changes in behavior. For each of the following edits, use the original version of the lablet as your starting point. In the space provided write down what error or behavior change you noted, and explain as best you can why the error or change was produced.

i. Change the statement in method `init` that reads:
```
cost = 75;
```

to read:
```
cost == 75;
```

ii. Change the statement in method `processQuarterButton` that reads:
```
amount += 25;
```

to read:
```
amount = amount + 25;
```

iii. Change the statement in method `processQuarterButton` that reads:
```
amount += 25;
```

to read:
```
amount = 25;
```

iv. Change the statement in function `processReturnButton` that reads:
```
int dollars = amount / 100;
```

to read:
```
float dollars = amount / 100;
```

v. Change the statement in function `processReturnButton` that reads:
```
int dollars = amount / 100;
```

to read:
```
int dollars = amount % 100;
```

vi. Change the statement in function `processReturnButton` that reads:
```
amountString=new String("$"+dollars + "." + pennies);
```

to read:
```
amountString=new String("$"+ dollars.valueOf() + "." +
                        pennies.valueOf());
```

vii. Change the phrase in class `ChoicePanel` that reads:
```
public Button colaButton,
```

to read:
```
private Button colaButton,
```

viii. Change the phrase in function `action` that reads:
```
else if (e.target == choices.colaButton)
```

to read:
```
else if (e.target == colaButton)
```

ix. Change the phrase in function `processColaButton` that reads:
```
choices.colaButton.disable();
```

to read:
```
colaButton.disable();
```

x. Change the phrase in class DispenserPanel that reads:
```
public  ChoicePanel()
```

to read:
```
private  ChoicePanel ()
```

2. To give you some practice using statements, let's make some changes to *SodaPop* that are pretty much direct extensions of its existing methods and classes.

a. Describe and implement a new type of soda. That is, extend *SodaPop* so that it displays and processes requests to dispense a fifth soda type.

b. Extend *SodaPop* so that in addition to the coins it can currently process, it also accepts dollar bills.

c. At present, our machine only returns change when the coin return button is pushed. That is, change is not returned automatically when a soda is dispensed, as it is on most real machines. Fix *SodaPop* so that it returns change (if excess money has been inserted) whenever a soda is dispensed.

d. The original applet keeps track of how many colas are in the machine, and signals when there are no colas left (by disabling the cola button). Fix the program so that it does comparable processing for all soda brands available.

e. In our applet, all types of soda cost that same. That is, there is one variable in our program to keep track of the cost for all items. Some vending machines dispense items that vary in price. Fix our machine so that it charges different prices for different types of soda.

3. There are many natural extensions that we could make to class `SodaPop` to enhance its functionality. Try each of the extensions listed below, one at a time. Compile and run your revised programs to test them out.

a. At present, an "exact change" indicator appears on the applet, but it is not implemented. Implement a simple version of a change counter as follows. Assume that the machine is initialized to have a small pot of money available for making change (say, $5.00), and that it only dispenses change from this pot. Once this change has all been dispensed, the exact change indicator should go on.

b. Now that our machine has a method for inserting dollar bills, let's make it realistic by having it reject half of the bills inserted. This can be accomplished by keeping a counter that is incremented each time a bill is inserted, and rejecting a bill when the counter, say, is even. One can check if a given int, `myCount`, is even using an `if` statement that begins `if ((myCount % 2) == 0)`.

c. In the original lablet, three panels are used to construct the applet as a whole. Panels `moneyPanel` and `insertCoinPanel` are internal (local) to the applet, but panel `choices` is implemented as an instance of a separate class, `ChoicePanel`. As we have seen in designing user interfaces, it is often advantageous to describe complex interfaces in terms of many separate classes. There is, though, some programming overhead associated with doing so. Change the program now so that each of the local panels, `moneyPanel` and `insertCoinPanel`, is implemented as a separate class. Then, make all required changes to the applet so that it uses these classes as it currently uses class `ChoicePanel`.

d. In the original lablet, class `ChoicePanel` is defined as a separate class. That class, though, is still described in the same file as is the *SodaPop* lablet. It need not be. Indeed, more complex Java programs are often implemented by collections of files, each describing one or more classes. Move class `ChoicePanel` to a separate file. Make all changes necessary so that the lablet runs as did the original.

Postlab Exercises

1. Design and implement a simple tax form, like those used by the IRS. You can design your own, or you can use a real form as a guide. In either case, your form should provide fields into which the user can enter information about, say, the number of deductions they are claiming, or their gross income. Then, when a "compute" button is pushed, some other computations should be performed based on the values entered.

CHAPTER 6

Events and Actions

Most of our lablets—indeed, most Java programs—take advantage of Java's facilities for producing graphical, user-friendly interfaces based on widgets and containers. Java's support for these "GUI" building blocks doesn't stop there, though. Built into every applet are the methods needed to make our widgets and containers respond to a full range of interface events. In this chapter we use two lablets to illustrate how one writes programs that not only display the interface elements that we want on the screen, but then actually respond to our button clicks, key presses, and mouse movements.

The first lablet, *GalaEvents,* is an extension (quite literally) of our lablet from Chapter 3, *Gigobite.* It demonstrates how to add event handlers to an existing applet so that the applet recognizes and responds to interface events. *GalaEvents* doesn't do much in response to these events, but at least it recognizes them. The second lablet, *SketchPad,* is a more full-blown example that not only recognizes interface events, but responds to them in interesting ways.

Lab Objectives

In this lab, you will:
- ❦ Run and experiment with class *GalaEvents,* to see the events that Java tracks for us and how to write code to control Java's responses to these events.
- ❦ Introduce some errors into *GalaEvents'* event handling routines, and see the effects of these changes.
- ❦ Run and experiment with the *SketchPad* lablet.
- ❦ Change *SketchPad* so that it responds differently to certain events.
- ❦ Extend *SketchPad* so that it recognizes and responds to some new events.

Exercises

1. Class `GalaEvents` extends class `Gigobite` (from the Chapter 3 lab exercises) to recognize many of Java's interface events, and to respond to them by printing out simple messages indicating what event occurred, where the event occurred, and, in some cases, what happened. To view these messages while the applet is running, make sure that variable VERBOSE is set to `true` before compiling the program. You may also have to open the "console" or "standard output" window. Check with your instructor for details on how to accomplish this in your Java programming environment.

    a. Compile and run *GalaEvents* now. Interact with the applet by using the mouse and the keyboard.

    b. For each of the events listed below, describe what you did to make that event occur. Be specific in your descriptions. That is, "I moved the mouse" doesn't explain too much. A more complete description would be something like "I dragged the mouse from outside of the applet window into the applet window and released the mouse button."

    　　i. `mouseEnter`

    　　ii. `mouseExit`

    　　iii. `mouseMove`

    　　iv. `mouseDrag`

    　　v. `mouseUp`

    　　vi. `mouseDown`

    　　vii. `action` (there are many ways to produce an action event)

    c. As usual, we'll modify the class `GalaEvents` now to induce some common errors and simple changes in behavior. For each of the following changes, use the original version of the lablet as your starting point. In the space provided write down what error or behavior change you noted, and explain as best you can why the error or change was produced.

i.   Remove the statement
```
return true;
```

from the `mouseUp` method

ii.   Remove the phrase
```
int x, int y
```

from the header of method `mouseDrag`

iii.   Remove the phrase
```
Event e
```

from the header of method `keyDown`

iv.   Remove the phrase
```
Object o
```

from the header of method `action`

v.   Change the phrase
```
(e.target==sandwiches)
```

in method `handleEvent` to read
```
(e.target = sandwiches)
```

(that is, change the "==" to an "=")

vi.   Change the phrase
```
(e.target==drinks)
```

in method `handleEvent` to read
```
e.target==drinks
```

(that is, remove the parentheses)

vii. Change the line in method `handleEvent` that reads:
```
else if (e.target == sides)
```

to read:
```
if (e.target == sides)
```

viii. Insert a ";" immediately after the header of method `mouseDrag` (between "`int y)`" and "`{`")

ix. Change the name of method `keyDown` to `keyUp`

2. The remainder of the exercises for this chapter refer to the *SketchPad* lablet. *SketchPad* is a very simple drawing program that allows you to draw arbitrary shapes on the screen using either the mouse (clicking and dragging) or the four cursor keys (left-arrow, right-arrow, up-arrow, and down-arrow) on your keyboard.

Compile and run *SketchPad* now. Use the applet to draw some designs on the screen. Use both the mouse and the cursor keys to control your drawing. Also, change the colors you use to draw.

3. Let's experiment a bit more aggressively with *SketchPad* now. Make the following changes, one at a time, to the original lablet, and record below the resulting changes in *SketchPad*'s behavior.

a. Remove the statement
```
currentColor = Color.black;
```

from method `init`. What happens? Why?

b. Move the declarations
```
private Button Clear;
private Checkbox color1, color2, color3, color4;
```

from their current locations, and place them at the start of method `init`. What happens? Why?

c. Remove (or just comment out) the lines in method `paint` that read:
```
startPoint.x = endPoint.x;
startPoint.y = endPoint.y;
```

What happens? Why?

d. Remove (or just "comment out") the entire `update` method. What happens? Why?

4. There are many natural extensions that we could make to the `SketchPad` class to enhance its functionality. Try each of the extensions listed below, one at a time. Compile and run your revised programs to test them out.

   a. The original applet allows you to use the cursor keys to draw anywhere—even outside of the applet window (although you can't see it!). The cursor can be directed with the cursor keys beyond the bounds of the applet window. Fix the program so that if one attempts to use the cursor keys to direct the cursor beyond the applet's bounds, nothing happens (that is, the cursor does not move outside of the applet window).

   b. At present, each keydown event causes the program to draw a line of a fixed size. Change the program so that if the Shift key is held down in conjunction with one of the cursor keys, a longer line is drawn (say, twice as long as in the case when the Shift key is not down).

   c. Extend *SketchPad* so that it allows erasing (that is, drawing in the same color as the background). Add a check box to the color controls that, when chosen, will accomplish erasing.

   d. *SketchPad* behaves unusually when one switches between using the mouse and the cursor keys. Specifically, if you click the mouse once in the applet window (without dragging it) and then hit a cursor key, a line is drawn connecting the point when the click occurred with the point where the cursor was previously. Fix this so that in this situation no line is drawn.

   e. Speaking of drawing lines, add a choice box to the control area on the screen which allows one to select between freehand drawing (as is currently done) and line drawing. When in line drawing mode, pushing the mouse button down indicates the starting points for drawing a line, the endpoints of which are determined by where the next `mouseUp` event occurs.

Postlab Exercises

1. Here is a slightly more adventurous—but still quite natural—extension of *SketchPad,* based on Exercise 4e, above. Expand *SketchPad* to allow the user to use the cursor to draw a variety of shapes, not just freehand drawings and lines. For example, you have seen that Java provides methods as part of its Graphics class for drawing rectangles, ovals, and the like. It even allows these shapes to be drawn "filled" with a color, or in outline (unfilled) form.

CHAPTER 7

Methodical Programming

Chapter 7 in the text is somewhat different from any of the others in that it is a review of what you've seen of Java so far. It offers very little in the way of new language features, concentrating instead on the details of using and defining methods. That's one reason we entitled it "Methodical Programming"—get it? The other reason we did so is that we wanted to devote a chapter to the programming process itself. We wanted to make as explicit as possible some of the practices we have been trying to convey implicitly through our sample programs and lablets about how to specify, design, implement, and test a program from scratch. In this sense, the chapter offers plenty of new ideas, and these are what you're going to focus on in this lab.

The "exercises" that follow are also quite different from those for any of the other chapters. First, and most obviously, there is no lablet here. Instead of providing you with a working sample program, we give you a vague, informal idea for a program, and leave it to you to take it from there. Also, rather than giving you directed tasks and problems to solve, we give you a checklist that will guide you through the process of program creation, dishing out some relevant pieces of advice along the way. In the process of creating your program, you will be developing the lablet and lab exercises for this chapter.

Lab Objectives

In this lab, you will:
- Develop a detailed program specification from an informal problem description.
- Design a collection of classes that describe your program.
- Define the methods needed to implement your classes.
- Use your programming environment to repeatedly write, test, and revise your program.

Exercises

1. We advised you in the text to make sure you know what you're supposed to do before beginning any programming task, and that's what we mean when we talk about specifying a program. At this point, your "specification" consists of the single statement: develop a 4-function calculator. Now, it's up to you to spell out the details. You don't need a computer to do this—you can use a paper and pencil to specify the look and operation of your program.

   a. Draw a picture of how you want your calculator to appear on the screen. You can use Figure 7.7 in the text as a starting point, or develop your own.

   b. Using the specification for our ATM program in section 7.2 of the text as a guide, describe the action of your program in terms of your visual design. That is, describe for each part of the interface what its role is.

   c. This is a good time to remember one particularly important piece of advice we offered in the text: The longer you put off coding, the better off you'll be in the long run. With this in mind, return to part (b) above, and make sure you have described the operation of your program to the extent that you can answer the following questions about it:

      i. What will happen when you click on the "5" key when the calculator's display is empty (or contains "0")? What about when the display already contains the number "17"? What about when it displays "24" as the result of a previous calculation (like after hitting "6 * 4 = ")?

      ii. What will happen when you click the "+" key? Is a calculation performed at that point? If so, which calculation?

      iii. What will happen if the first key clicked is the "−" key?

      iv. Will your program be able to process sequences of operations like real calculators can? That is, what will your program do in response to a series of clicks, like "5 + 4 − 3 * 2 ="?

      v. If your program includes keys for "C" and "CE", what is the difference between them?

d.   Before moving on, you should ask yourself if you can seen how to expand your program to accomplish any other common calculator tasks (like a one-number memory, or built-in unary operations, such as square root). If so, you may want to incorporate these features into your specification now, and leave them unimplemented until you're ready to deal with them.

2.   Your goal in designing a program us to identify and describe the classes you will need to accomplish its processing goals, and to have a first crack at implementing them. With this in mind, it behooves you to answer the following.

a.   What classes are suggested by the picture you developed in Exercise 1a?

b.   Have you seen examples of classes that are similar (or identical!) to any of those you listed? If so, which ones? For each such class, decide if it can be incorporated directly into your program, or if it will have to be modified to match your program's specification.

c.   Can any of the widgets or classes you have identified be combined into containers and described as new classes? For each container you will use, describe in the space below which widgets and objects it will contain, and which layout manager it will use.

d.   Starting with your applet, implement the interface portion (don't worry about the `action` methods—for the time being they can just be stubs) for each of the classes you have identified. Add them one at a time to your applet framework, compiling, debugging, and re-compiling as you go.

e.   Even after it compiles and produces the desired interface, it is worth looking over your program as it now stands to consider questions like the following. If the answer to any of them is "No," "I don't know," or "HELP!," that is probably grounds for reconsidering at least one of your previous responses.

   i.   Can you name every component that your program will refer to? In particular, write out the full name used to reference the "3" key, the "=" key, and the number display.

   ii.   Are all data members properly described as either `private` or `public`? Add these descriptors now.

        iii. Can you identify the major public methods that will be part of each class? You should be able, at the very least, to write stubs for these methods with appropriate signatures. For example, write the applet's action method and have it refer to methods like "processPlus," "processMinus," "processTimes," and "processDivide."

        iv. Are there any other obvious private helper methods that you can already see a need for? Write the code (or write stubs) for any such methods.

3. Filling in the coding details for your classes always requires care and thought, but it shouldn't inflict inordinate pain on the programmer if one is systematic in going about it. Start writing your methods now, keeping the following pieces of advice in mind.

    a. Keep your Java documentation handy at all times. You can use it to remind yourself about syntactic details, and to find descriptions of built-in classes and methods that will support your coding efforts.

    b. Write the easiest methods first. If a method turns out to be complicated, leave it in stub form, and return to it after working on other related methods.

    c. If any method becomes long enough or confusing enough that it can't easily be explained, write some private helper methods to encapsulate some of its processing.

    d. If a sequence of code is used in more than one place in your program, encapsulate that code in a private helper method.

    e. As you define your methods, test them out immediately. Try to identify and isolate any errors before adding too much new code to a working program.

4. There are a number of "clean up" activities that should always be performed, even after a program runs to your satisfaction. Do each of these now, before "releasing" your program to the public (or, your instructor).

    a. Even though you have been testing your program out as you have been writing it, it is always a good idea to have someone else run it to see if they detect any problems. Give your program to one of your classmates, and have them run it. Record and address any errors that they encounter and any behavior that they take issue with.

b. Review the original specification you developed for the program to convince yourself that the program performs "according to spec."

c. Now, review the code itself with an eye towards style. If there are any statements that are unnecessary, variables or data members that are unused, or statement that were added for the purpose of testing your program, remove them now. Be sure to test your program afterwards, to make sure nothing of importance was removed by mistake.

d. We told you to make note of any obvious extensions that could be made to your program in your program specification. If any of these seem particularly straightforward to you, implement them now. See the Postlab Exercises below for some suggestions.

e. Finally, check to see that your code is completely and clearly documented. At the very least, every class and method should be described to the extent that its role in the overall processing scheme is clear. If it's not clear to you what a particular statement or method is doing, imagine how confusing it will be to someone else who must read your code—like your instructor!

Postlab Exercises

1. Add a one-number memory to your calculator, and keys that will allow you to clear, recall, add to, and subtract from memory.

2. Extend your program to be a scientific calculator. That is, add keys for calculating a variety of unary functions. See Java's Math class for some ideas about what would be easy to implement.

3. Change your calculator so that it looks like a graphing calculator by adding a second display to use for drawing graphs and a "graph" button that, when clicked, displays a simple graph in the new display. Doing any actual graphing of functions would require a complete overhaul of the calculator, so only attempt that if you're *very* ambitious.

CHAPTER 8

Collections

The lablet for Chapter 8, based on class `Sortmeister`, not only demonstrates a couple of standard sorting algorithms, but also displays the data items being sorted graphically. It uses one array to store the integers being sorted, and another to describe the text fields that hold the integer values. It uses `String` objects and operations to manipulate the data in the text fields, and a variety of iterative statements (loops) to control the processing involved in sorting and displaying the data. In short, it does a great job of illustrating the power and utility of all of the Java features that are introduced in this chapter.

Lab Objectives

In this lab, you will:
- Run the *Sortmeister* lablet, and watch it sort random lists of integers using two standard sorting algorithms.
- Edit the applet to induce some simple errors related to arrays, strings, and loops.
- Change the applet in simple ways to vary how it accomplishes the sorting and displaying of data.
- Extend the applet to implement some additional sorting algorithms.

Exercises

1. We'll start, as usual, by running the lablet and watching it in its current working condition. Then, we'll play around with it to illustrate some common mistakes in dealing with arrays and loops.

    Compile and run *Sortmeister* now. Click on the applet's "Reset" button to load new integer values, and then sort them by clicking "Sort". You can determine which sorting algorithm is used by choosing either "Selection" or "Shell" from the choice box provided.

2. The lablet makes extensive use of arrays and loops, in almost all phases of its processing. Let's focus on these features as we introduce some errors into the applet. Some of the changes listed below will result in compiler errors. Others will not keep the applet from compiling, but will cause it to run differently or incorrectly. Make each of these changes to the original version of *Sortmeister,* and then record what happens when you try to compile and run the revised applet.

    a. Change the line that reads:
        ```
        private int data[];
        ```

        to read:
        ```
        private int data;
        ```

    b. Change the line that reads:
        ```
        private TextField display[];
        ```

        to read:
        ```
        private TextField display [SIZE];
        ```

    c. Change the line in method `init` that reads:
        ```
        data = new int[SIZE];
        ```

        to read:
        ```
        data = new int[];
        ```

    d. Delete (or comment out) the line in method `init` that reads:
        ```
        display[i] = new TextField(3);
        ```

e.   Remove the left brace that appears after the line in method `init` that reads:
```
for(int i=0; i<SIZE; i++)
```

and, remove the right brace that appears before the line in function `init` that reads:
```
this.add("West", p1);
```

f.   Change the line in method `init` that reads:
```
for(int i=0; i<SIZE; i++)
```

to read:
```
for(int i=1; i<SIZE; i++)
```

g.   Change the line in method `paint` that reads:
```
for(int i=0; i < SIZE; i++)
```

to read:
```
for(int i=0; i <= SIZE; i++)
```

h.   Change the line in method `paint` that reads:
```
display[i].setText("" + data[i]);
```

to read:
```
display[i].setText(data[i]);
```

i.   Change the line in method `processResetButton` that reads:
```
data[i] = (int) (Math.random() * DATA_MAX);
```

to read:
```
data[i] = (Math.random() * DATA_MAX);
```

j.   Remove "[]" from the header of method `selectionSort`

k.   Change the line in method `ShellSort` that reads:
```
while (increment >= 1)
```

to read:
```
while (increment > 1)
```

3.   Here are some relatively straightforward changes to the program—that is, they can be made without disrupting the structure of the original applet. Try them one at a time. Compile and run your revised applets to test them out.

a. Change the applet so that sorting (using either algorithm) produces a list of numbers in descending (as opposed to ascending) order.

b. Rewrite function `ShellSort` to use a do statement instead of `while` statement to control its outermost loop.

c. Add a "Clear" button to the applet which when clicked resets all data values back to zero and redraws the screen accordingly.

4. The extensions described below are a bit more adventurous than those above in that they involve changes to both the algorithms and the user interface of the lablet. Try these one at a time, and run your revised applet to test them out.

a. Add another sorting algorithm to the list of available algorithms, and implement the algorithm. Look up any established sorting algorithm, or develop one of your own.

b. The original version of the lablet does its job, and looks pretty good doing it. If our program is really going to help us "visualize" the algorithm, it should show us clearly the intermediate results of sorting the array, which tell us a lot about how the algorithm is working. The real problem with getting your program to show clearly its intermediate results is one of speed. The program works so quickly that, even when we try to see what's happening during sorting, it's tough to detect anything. So, what we want to do is slow the program down enough so that we can see the sorting in progress.

There are two easy ways to slow our program down. One is to have the program stop, or at least waste some time, every time it goes to switch some elements around. This can be accomplished by inserting "do-nothing" for-loops at strategic points in the program. We have provided a method that does this for you, creating delays of length DELAY. Adjust the value of class variable DELAY so that you can see the sorting in progress.

c. The second way to slow the program down is simply to increase the size of the array it is sorting. The only difficulty with doing this in the context of Sortmeister is that the program uses text fields to display String versions of all data. These fields take up space on the applet panel, and can only be made so small—not small enough to accommodate, say, an array of 100 elements. The key is to get rid of the text fields, and display the data strictly in graphical form (that is, just as lines of varying length, and not as numbers). This will allow you to increase the array size to, say, 100.

Make these changes now, so that we can really see *Sortmeister* in action.

Postlab Exercises

1. Using class *Sortmeister* as a model, write an applet that sorts a list of words. Allow the user to enter arbitrary strings of characters into a series of text fields, and then rearrange the strings to put them into alphabetical order.

2. Write an applet that shuffles a deck of cards, and then "deals" them one at a time. You can represent cards by character strings (for example, "2d" for 2 of diamonds, and "Qh" for queen of hearts). As usual when you have a new data type, you might consider writing a class Card, whose objects are individual cards.

CHAPTER 9

Exceptions

The Chapter 9 lablet, based on class *OrderPlease,* is interesting for a couple of reasons. First of all, despite its length, it doesn't really do much. It presents to its user an increasingly common electronic order form to be filled out, and when directed to do so, "submits" the order by simply printing the order information on the screen as it might appear on a shipping label. What little processing is done (the adding of an item to an order, the resetting of the order form, and the submitting of the order) is quite simple. It takes a good deal of code, though, to describe all of the components and containers that make up the applet's interface.

The most interesting feature of the lablet—and the reason that we are using it in this chapter—is that it makes good use of Java's Exception subclasses to ensure that any errors or omissions made by the user in entering information are caught before an order is processed. Using exceptions can improve radically the "usability" of an applet, particularly in cases like this where the user is required to enter a lot of information that is critical to the operation of the program. The exercises that follow will focus on how the lablet uses exceptions to produce a "safer" program.

Lab Objectives

In this lab, you will:
- Run and test this chapter's lablet, *OrderPlease,* paying particular attention to how it detects and responds to user errors.
- Edit the lablet to cause some typical syntax errors related to exceptions.
- Add some new exception handling features to the applet.

Exercises

1. We typically ask you to start each set of lab exercises by running the corresponding lablet, and that is what we'll so here. Unlike previous labs, though, we want you to try to induce errors into this lablet's processing by entering some nonsensical data, and by omitting some necessary data, rather than just modifying the applet's code. *OrderPlease* reports its order and error processing in the standard output (or, console) window, so make sure that it is visible before starting the applet.

   a. First, compile and run *OrderPlease* as you would if you were using it to order merchandise from Monty's Musical Madness. Enter realistic data for all of the information requested, and submit your order.

   b. Clear the order form by clicking the Reset button. Then, try the following operations. Record what happens in each case, and use the program listing (we've included only the parts of the lablet that relate directly to exceptions) to explain why.

      i. See if you can add -5 (that's negative 5!) Harmonious Harmonicas to your new order.

      ii. Enter "abc" as a quantity for a "Going Going Gong", and try to add that item to your order.

      iii. Add some legitimate items to an order, but leave some information, like the credit card number, blank. Try submitting the order.

   c. Let's edit the program to remove one of its exception handling sections, and then re-run the program to see what the exceptions are preventing.

      i. Comment out the try-catch clause in function `processAddItemButton` leaving only the statements:
         ```
         int quantity=Integer.parseInt(custQuantity.getText());
         doAddItem(quantity);
         ```

      ii. Compile and run the edited program.

      iii. Enter "abc" as the quantity for any item, and try to add that item to your order.

2. Make the following edits to the original version of the lablet, one at a time. For each, try to compile and run the revised applet, recording what happened and why.

    a. Remove "ex" from the line in function `processAddItemButton` that reads:
```
catch (NumberFormatException ex)
```

    b. Change the line in function `processAddItemButton` that reads:
```
catch (IllegalQuantity ex)
```
     to read:
```
catch (Ilegalquantity ex)
```

    c. Replace the statements in function `action` that read:
```
try
{
    processSubmitButton();
}
catch (MissingData ex) // Some data was missing
{
    order.appendText("*** " + ex.getMessage() + CRLF);
    repaint();
}
```
     with:
```
processSubmitButton();
```

    d. Remove the phrase "`throws  IllegalQuantity`" from the header of function `doAddItem`

    e. Change the header of function `processSubmitButton` to read:
```
private void processSubmitButton() throws MIssingdata
```

3. Even with *OrderPlease*'s current level of exception handling, it still doesn't take much to submit an order that is bogus for one reason or another. Let's make some interesting extensions to the applet in the interest of plugging some of the remaining security gaps. In each case, you will have to:

    • define a new `Exception` class,
    • decide where instances of the exception should be thrown from,
    • decide where to catch the exception, and finally,
    • determine what processing should be done when the exception is caught.

a.   The original lablet allows one to enter any data at all for a zip code. Fix the program so that it will not submit an order that does not have a legal zip code. For our purposes, we'll assume that any integer in the range of 10000-99999 could be a legal zip code.

b.   The original applet asks the user to specify an expiration date for the credit card being used. Unfortunately, an expired card is accepted just as readily as an active one. Fix the program so that it will not submit an order unless the credit card expiration data is sometime in the future. To simplify things, we'll assume that all that is to be entered into this field is the year of expiration (in full numeric form, e.g., 1997), and that any card with a year that is greater than or equal the current year is acceptable.

Postlab Exercises

1.   As we described earlier, much of the code in *OrderPlease* is devoted to describing the many components and containers in the applet's interface. One common pair of components is a label and a text field, where the label describes the information to be entered in the text field.

a.   Write a class `LabelledTextField`, which extends class `Panel` and holds a label and a text field. The class should define methods for constructing labelled text fields (blank ones, and ones with predefined labels), for setting the text in the text field, and for getting the text (as a String) from it.

b.   Edit class `OrderPlease` to use class `LabelledTextField` wherever it is appropriate.

c.   Extend class `LabelledTextField` to create a class `LabelledIntTextField`. A `LabelledIntTextField` is a `LabelledTextField` that is designed to hold only integer values. Add exception handling to class `LabelledIntTextField` to detect and prevent any attempt to set an object's text to a non-integer value.

CHAPTER 10

Input/Output

Historically, the phrase "input-output" (or, "I/O") referred to the operations involved in securing input data from a keyboard and displaying information on a screen or printer. As file processing became prevalent in the early years of computing, I/O was expanded to encompass using disk files for input and output. In today's world of graphical user interfaces, the term I/O has been expanded even further to include all of the operations involved in communicating between a computer and its users. As we have already seen, these operations include retrieving text that has been entered into text containers and processing the text using Java's built-in string classes.

In this lablet we present you with a remarkably simple, but remarkably realistic, word-processing program (described as class WordPro) that illustrates many of these facets of I/O. *WordPro* also illustrates the use of three additional Java features that we have yet to explore. First, the class WordPro is not an applet, but is another type of container called a frame. This means that we describe the class in terms of a constructor function and a main member function. It also means that the *WordPro* program cannot be embedded in a WWW page, for example, but can be run as a stand-alone "application." Second, we chose to make WordPro a frame so that we could attach a menu bar to it (which we can't do to an applet). So, the program shows you how to describe and respond to menu choices. Finally, because we wanted to make this program handle file I/O in a familiar way, we make use of Java's class that implements file dialog boxes. Other than that, nothing is new.

Lab Objectives

In this lab, you will:

❦ Run the Chapter 10 lablet, *WordPro*, and exercise its text handling capabilities.

❦ Introduce some common errors into *WordPro* that relate to its use of frames, menus, files, and dialogs.

❦ Extend the lablet to implement a variety of common word-processing operations.

Exercises

1. Maybe you expect this by now, but when we first ran this lablet we were struck by how (relatively) easy it was to produce a realistic version of what appears to be a very complex program in only a few pages of Java code. Whether you're impressed or not, there is no denying that class WordPro looks familiar to anyone who uses a modern WYSIWYG (short for "What You See Is What You Get") word-processing program.

a. Compile and run *WordPro* now. Compare what you see on the screen with the code for the WordPro class's constructor function, shown here. Make sure you understand which parts of the code are responsible for which parts of the program's interface.

```
public class WordPro extends Frame
{
    String clipBoard = new String("");
    TextArea text = new TextArea(20,80);

    public WordPro()
    {
        setTitle("p.j WordPro");
        // Declare the menu bar for this frame
        MenuBar mbar = new MenuBar();
        // Define and add the File menu to the menu bar
        Menu m = new Menu("File");
        m.add(new MenuItem("New"));
        m.add(new MenuItem("Open"));
        m.add(new MenuItem("Close"));
        m.addSeparator();
        m.add(new MenuItem("Save"));
        m.add(new MenuItem("Save As..."));
        m.addSeparator();
        m.add(new MenuItem("Quit"));
```

```
        mbar.add(m);
        // Define and add the Edit menu to the menu bar
        m = new Menu("Edit");
        m.add(new MenuItem("Cut"));
        m.add(new MenuItem("Copy"));
        m.add(new MenuItem("Delete"));
        m.add(new MenuItem("Paste"));
        mbar.add(m);
        // Attach the menu bar and add the text area to our frame
        // Remember, frames use Border layout
        setMenuBar(mbar);
        add("South", display);
        add("Center",text);
    }
```

b. Now, try using the program. It operates much as you would expect, with a few minor exceptions. You can type text into the window and edit it using the keyboard. You can cut, copy, delete, and paste text by selecting text and using the commands in the Edit menu. Choosing "New" from the File menu clears the text window. Experiment with these features of WordPro until you are comfortable with them.

c. Select "Open..." from the File menu and choose any text file (it could even be one of your Java source files) to open. Edit the file to indicate that it has been opened and edited by WordPro. Then, chose "Save" from the File menu to save your edited file. Choose "Open..." again to look at the new, edited file.

2. Let's make some simple changes to *WordPro* now, and observe the effects of these changes. As you have done in other labs, make each change listed to the original program, and record in the space provided what error or change in behavior occurred when you tried to compile and run the program.

a. Change the header of function main to read:
```
private static void main(String args[])
```

b. Change the header of function main to read:
```
public static void main()
```

c. Remove (or comment out) the statement in function main that reads:
```
myFrame.show();
```

d. Remove (or comment out) one of the statement in the WordPro constructor that reads:
```
mbar.add(m);
```

e. Remove (or comment out) the statement in the constructor that reads:
```
setMenuBar(mbar);
```

f. Remove (or comment out) the statement in function doOpen that reads:
```
myFD.show();
```

g. Remove (or comment out) the statement in function doOpen that reads:
```
processNewMenu();
```

h. Remove (or comment out) the statement in function doOpen that reads:
```
inStream.close();
```

i. Change the line in function doOpen that reads:
```
text.appendText(textLine + "\n");
```

to read:
```
text.appendText(textLine);
```

j. Remove (or comment out) the statement in function doSave that reads:
```
DataOutputStream outStream = new DataOutputStream(fos);
```

k. Change the line in function doSave that reads:
```
fileName = dir + File.separator + name;
```

to read:
```
fileName = dir + name;
```

l. Change the line in function doDelete that reads:
```
String s1 = new String
        (all.substring(0,text.getSelectionStart()));
```

to read:
```
String s1 = new String
        (all.substring(1,text.getSelectionStart()));
```

m. Reverse the order of the two statements in method action that occur immediately after the statement:
```
else if (arg.equals("Cut"))
```

3. Return now to the original version of *WordPro*. It provides us with examples of code that can be used to implement a number of features that will render our word-processor even more realistic—and functional—than it already is. Some of the changes we propose can be made without changing the existing user interface at all. Others require that your first add some components to the interface, and then implement them. Given that these extensions tend to build upon one another, you should attempt them in the prescribed order.

a. Most word processors change the title of their text window to reflect the name of the file currently being edited (and use "Untitled" for documents that have not previously been saved). Fix *WordPro* so that it does this.

b. Implement the Close command from *WordPro's* File menu. For now, this operation can have the same effect as the New menu command does.

c. Add to the menu bar a Font menu that specifies a few type faces. Then, implement it so that when a type face is chosen, all text in the window is displayed in the chosen font.

d. Implement the Save as... command from the File menu. This should present the user with a file dialog box that allows the user to name the file to be used for saving the document.

e. Add a Find command to the Edit menu. Implement Find so that it prompts the user via a dialog box for a string, and then searches the current document for the first occurrence of that string.

f. Most modern word processors are "safe" in the sense that, for example, if you choose New, Open, or Close from the File menu, and there is currently "dirty" text in the text window (that is, text that has been changed since the current file was opened), you will be asked (via a dialog box) if you want to save the current text before performing any of these operations. Extend WordPro to act more safely when responding to these commands.

Postlab Exercises

1. Write a class `Keyboard` which performs basic, type-specific input operations through the standard system input-output window. That is, your class should implement the following functions, which could be used by any other program to accomplish a traditional style of keyboard input.

```
public static void prompt(String s);
// prompts the user with String s,
// in the standard I/O window

public static int readInt(String s);
// prompts the user with String s,
// then, reads and returns a single integer

public static double readDouble(String s);
// prompts the user with String s,
// then, reads and returns a single double

public static String readLine(String s);
// prompts the user with String s,
// then, reads and returns a line of text up to a return

public static String readWord(String s);
// prompts the user with String s,
// then, reads and returns a word as delimited
// by a space or a return
```

2 .   Return to the Chapter 9 lablet, *OrderPlease.* Whenever an exception was encountered in *OrderPlease* a message was posted in text form to the System output window. A more realistic way of reporting such errors is by means of a dialog box that must be acknowledged by "clicking" it away. Extend *OrderPlease* to make use of dialog boxes when reporting exceptions.

CHAPTER 11

Threads

Java is not the first programming language to support multi-threading. It is, though, the first to provide direct language support for both threads and the graphical user interface tools (in the Abstract Window Toolkit) that we have used to develop all of our lablets. This combination allows us to write programs that are responsive to their users in ways that are not easily achieved using other languages. In essence, we can now write programs that are capable of responding to user interface events while they are performing some other processing.

In the case of this chapter's lablet, *TickTock,* we have what appears to be a simple implementation of a modern digital alarm clock. What is interesting about it from a programming standpoint is that the program actually performs like a real clock. That is to say, while it is busy displaying and updating the current time, it is still responsive to button clicks which can interrupt this processing. When alternate processing, like setting the alarm, is completed, the program returns to its regular processing without a hitch. This, of course, is all made possible by the fact that TickTock uses a thread.

In the exercises that follow we'll analyze and experiment with *TickTock's* use of threads, and we'll extend it to accomplish more threaded behavior.

Lab Objectives

In this lab, you will:
- Run and experiment with the Chapter 11 lablet, *TickTock*, to understand its operation.
- Analyze the lablet's use of threads and how they affect its performance.

❦   Extend the lablet to implement another threaded mode of behavior, a chronometer.

Exercises

1.   We start, as usual, by running our lablet. The good news is that the operation of the *TickTock* program is very realistic in that it operates much like a modern digital clock or watch might. The bad news is that as a result of this realism our program is every bit as confusing to use (at first glance, anyhow) as is any new digital clock. Your first job, then, is to run the program and to use it enough so that you understand how it works. We'll offer the following hint to get you going: The clock has two modes, time mode and alarm mode.

   a.   Compile and run *TickTock* now. Notice which buttons have been enabled and which have been disabled as you run it. Then, click on whatever buttons are enabled, and see what happens. Try setting the alarm. Once you see how to do this, set the alarm for some time in the very near future (making sure that you take the AM/PM indicator into account, and return to clock mode. Keep track of what happens every time you click on something.

   b.   Just as with real clocks, there are two ways to figure out how *TickTock* operates. One is to start playing with it, as in part (a). The other is to RTFM ("read the fabulous manual"). We have provided you with a simple user's manual in the text. Read through that now, to make sure you didn't miss any of *TickTock's* features.

   c.   Now, compare your users' manual with the portions of *TickTock's* code to see how your descriptions are reflected in the lablet.

2.   Let's experiment more directly with the lablet's code to see how it uses threads to accomplish its processing. You know the drill. Make each of these changes to the original version of *TickTock,* and record the impact of the change. Note in each case what type of error occurred (if one occurred at all) and/or what change in program behavior resulted from the change. Be forewarned that some of these changes produce very subtle differences in behavior. In some cases, you may have to click some buttons to detect the differences.

a.   Remove (or comment out) the phrase from the header of class `Timer` that reads:
```
implements Runnable
```

b.   Remove (or comment out) the entire header and body of `Timer`'s `start` method.

c.   Change the body of `Timer`'s `start` method to read:
```
clockThread = new Thread(this);
clockThread.start();
```

(that is, eliminate the surrounding `if` statement).

d.   Change the statement in `Timer`'s `start` method that reads:
```
clockThread = new Thread(this);
```

to read:
```
clockThread = new Thread();
```

e.   Remove the phrase from `Timer`'s `run` method that reads:
```
while(clockThread != null) {
```

and the next-to-last closing brace ("`}`") from method `run`.

f.   Change the body of method `updateTime` to read:
```
hour = h;
minute = m;
second = s;
repaint();
```

(that is, eliminate the surrounding `if` statement).

g.   Change the line in method `run` that reads:
```
Thread.sleep(250);
```

to read:
```
clockThread.sleep(250);
```

h.   Change the line in `Timer`'s `run` method that reads:
```
Thread.sleep(250);
```

to read:
```
Thread.sleep(1);
```

      i.   Remove (or comment out) the `try` and `catch` clauses in `Timer`'s `run` method surrounding the line that reads:

            `Thread.sleep(250);`

      j.   Remove (or comment out) the entire `try` and `catch` clause—including the `Thread.sleep` statement— from `Timer`'s `run` method.

3. Return now to the original version of the lablet so that we can extend it to perform even more realistically. While each of the following extensions is independent of the others, their ordering reflects their relative difficulty. So, we recommend that you do them in the order presented.

      a.   When the original lablet is in "alarm" mode, it displays the time in the same format it uses when in "clock" mode—that is, in "hour:minute:second" format. Normally, when setting an alarm, one isn't too concerned about the seconds. Fix the program so that when *TickTock* is in alarm mode, it only displays the hours and minutes, and not the seconds.

      b.   At present, we can set *TickTock's* alarm, but nothing much happens when the alarm time matches the current time. Fix the program so that if the alarm has been set, and the alarm time matches the current time, the program switches to alarm mode (displaying the alarm time) to indicate that the alarm "went off."

      c.   Add a chronometer to our clock that can be started, and continues to display the elapsed time, even when in clock or alarm modes, until it is explicitly stopped. There are many ways to accomplish this, and we leave it to you to decide how you want to tackle this. Any approach that we can think of entails some re-design of *TickTock,* since it presently only recognizes two modes of operation, and doesn't provide an easy way for getting, say, from alarm mode to chronometer mode.

Postlab Exercises

1. Return to the lablet from Chapter 8, *Sortmeister.* We mentioned that one of its shortcomings is that the sorting process happens too quickly to be seen in action. As we described, one way to slow the process down is by introducing empty loops. Another way we can now see is to use a thread to control the sorting, and to put the thread to sleep when we want to slow things down. Rewrite class `Sortmeister` so that it uses threads to help visualize the sorting.

2. Threads can be used to make *Sortmeister* even more revealing about comparative sorting algorithms. Rewrite *Sortmeister* now so that two sort algorithms can be applied to the same data and we can compare their performance side-by-side. That is, have your new program create two "sorting displays," each executing a different algorithm on the same original data.

CHAPTER 12

Applets in Cyberspace

As we described in the text, the lablets for this chapter tie together nearly all of the Java language features and the programming topics that we have discussed throughout the book. These programs make use of most of Java's statements and standard classes, as well as arrays, packages, inheritance, exceptions, and threads, all in the realistic context of creating graphical and animated buttons. The resulting classes are written generally so that they can be used directly in any future programs that you write. So, by completing this last set of exercises you will have reached the point where you can implement useful, re-usable, "industrial-strength" widgets of your own devising (with a little help from us).

The new material that is illustrated here, dealing primarily with Java's multimedia classes, also represents an interesting closure because it presents Java in its original intended context: as a language for writing programs for the Worldwide Web. The relationship between Java and HTML is, at long last, made explicit here, and the virtues of the aforementioned language features become more obvious than ever.

Lab Objectives

In this lab, you will:
- View the two lablets for this chapter from within a single HTML page.
- See how we can provide parameters to an applet using HTML, and how applets access and make use of parameters.
- Experiment with the parts of the lablets that use the `Image` and `MediaTracker` classes.
- Extend both lablets to do more advanced image processing.

Exercises

1. Typically, we ask you to start a set of lab exercises by running the lablet for the chapter, and this last chapter is no different in that regard. What is different is that there are two lablets to run. You could compile and run each one separately, but we've already provided you with everything you need to view both applets in action at once. The Chapter 12 folder on the `programming.java` lab disk contains an HTML file and all of the class and image files you need to get going.

    a. Look at the listing of file "example1.html" (you have soft copy of it on your disk). This is the file that is described in Section 12.4 of the text. It contains two APPLET elements, one referring to our first lablet ("OldButtoner"), and the other referring to our second lablet ("Buttoner"). Viewing this file will effectively run both lablets and display them on the same browsed page. Do so now. Click on the buttons to watch them do their stuff.

    b. Not only do we have two lablets referenced from a single HTML file, but our lablets are composed of four classes, a collection of image files (with ".gif" extensions), and a `package`. It is important before we start working with these programs that you understand the relationships between all of the files involved. Answer these questions:

        i. What is `myWidgets`?

        ii. What does `myWidgets` contain?

        iii. Which files use `myWidgets`? How does each file use it?

        iv. What type of object is `OldButtoner`?

        v. `OldButtoner` refers to which of our buttons, `GraphicButton` or `AnimatedButton`?

        vi. As it is currently invoked from "example1.html," which image files are used by `OldButtoner`?

        vii. What type of object is `Buttoner`?

      viii. Which of our button classes does `Buttoner` refer to?

      ix. In Java terms, what is the relationship between `GraphicButton` and `AnimatedButton`?

      x. In English, describe the relationship between `GraphicButton` and `AnimatedButton`?

2. Before we begin experimenting with the Java code that implements our new buttons, let's look more closely at the HTML code that we're using to invoke our applets. By changing the parameter values that we provide for the applets, we can illustrate many of their features and capabilities. Make each of the following changes, one at a time, to the original version of "example1.html". Then, record and explain how the applet responded to the change.

    a. Change the value of *OldButtoner's* "label" parameter to "Graphic".

    b. Change the value of *Buttoner's* "label" parameter to "Animate".

    c. Remove the "label" parameter from both `APPLET` elements.

    d. Change the value of *OldButtoner's* "numPix" parameter to "5".

    e. Change the value of *OldButtoner's* "numPix" parameter to "1".

    f. Change the value of *OldButtoner's* "pattern" parameter to "wrong*.gif".

    g. Change the value of *Buttoner's* "pattern" parameter to "ab*.gif".

    h. Change the value of parameter "destURL" to any legal URL that you know, like for your personal home page. If you don't know any others, you can use the value "`http://www.hamilton.edu/html/academic/Compsci`".

3. Now, in our more customary way, we ask you to make some changes to the Java code for our lablets. We will concentrate, as you would expect, on those language features that implement the lablet's abilities to process applet parameters and images. Make these changes to the original version of the indicated file, and record and explain either the resulting error, or the change in behavior.

Make the following changes to class `OldButtoner`:

a. Remove the line that reads:
```
import myWidgets.*;  // for GraphicButton
```

b. Change the line in function `init` that reads:
```
numImgs = getIntParameter("numPix", 2);
```

to read:
```
numImgs = getIntParameter("numPix", 0);
```

c. Change the line in function `init` that reads:
```
theLabel    = getParameter("label");
```

to read:
```
theLabel    = getParameter("myLabel");
```

d. Remove the lines in function `loadImages` that read
```
try
    tracker.waitForID(i);
catch (InterruptedException e);
```

e. Change the line in function `getParameterInfo` that starts
```
String[][] aboutParams
```

to start with
```
String[] aboutParams = {
```

f. Remove the open brace ("{") from the line in function `getParameterInfo` that reads:
```
String[][] aboutParams = {
```
and one of the close braces ("}") from the line that reads:
```
{"destURL",    "URL","destination when clicked"}};
```

Make the following changes to class `GraphicButton`:

g. Change the line that reads:
```
protected Image[] theImage; //0 -> is down,
```

to read:
```
private Image[] theImage;   //0 -> is down,
```

h. Change the line that reads:
```
protected int curImage = 1;
```

to read:
```
protected int curImage = 0;
```

i. Remove (or comment out) the line in function `fitLabel` that reads:
```
FontMetrics fm = getFontMetrics(getFont());
```

j. Change the line in function `fitLabel` that reads:
```
labelBase = (thisHeight+fm.getAscent() - fm.getDescent())/ 2;
```

to read:
```
labelBase = (thisHeight+fm.getAscent() - fm.getDescent());
```

k. Remove (or comment out) the line in function `mouseUp` that reads:
```
postEvent(new Event(this, Event.ACTION_EVENT, theLabel));
```

Make the following change to class `Buttoner`:

l. Change the line in function init that reads:
```
theButton = new AnimatedButton(images, theLabel, 100);
```

to read:
```
theButton = new AnimatedButton(images, theLabel, 0);
```

4. It is time, at last, to make some more substantive changes to the original version of our lablets, ones that will extend their behavior in more useful ways. As usual, we ask you to make the proposed extensions one at a time, testing them out as you go. Since they build upon one another, do them in the order listed.

a. As currently implemented, class `GraphicButton` changes the button's image very quickly. When the mouse goes down over the button, the image changes, but it is changed back immediately when the mouse is released. Change `GraphicButton` so that it produces a "locking button"—one that "goes down" when clicked, and stays that way until it is clicked again, when it "pops up."

b. Now, extend class `GraphicButton` so that the button it produces is disabled when it is in the "down" state. That is, clicking on it when it is already "down" should not direct you to a new URL, but should merely "pop the button up," by changing its image and enabling it.

c. At present, our `AnimatedButton` "bounces through" the images used to represent its "up" state. That is, if we provide a total of 5 images for an animated button (image 0 to be used for the "down" state, and images 1-4 for its "up" state), it displays the "up" images in the order: 1, 2, 3, 4, 3, 2, 1, 2, 3, 4, 3, 2, 1, ... Change the algorithm so that animated images cycle through their "up" images, displaying our 4 images in this order: 1, 2, 3, 4, 1, 2, 3, 4, 1, 2, 3, 4... .

d. If we want them to perform as advertised, we must provide two images to be used in rendering a `GraphicButton`, and at least three for an `AnimatedButton`. Let's try to simplify things for the users of our classes, as follows.

    i. Change class `GraphicButton` so that it accepts a single image as a parameter (you can use the value of the "pattern" parameter to specify the file name for the image, and can get rid of the "numPix" parameter). Then, have `GraphicButton` use a `FadeFilter`, as described in Exercise 12 of the text, to create a grayed-out version of the image that will be displayed for the button's "down" state.

    ii. Change class `AnimatedButton` so that it, too, requires only a single image as its "pattern" parameter. It should, like the revised `GraphicButton` above, use a `FadeFilter` to produce the image to be used for the button's "down" state. The "up" states for the animated button should be produced be repositioning the button's label. That is, the image for the animated button will not change when the button is "up," but the position of the label will. So, an animated button with a "label" value of "Hi!" might cycle through four animated images as follows.

Postlab Exercises

1. You may have already noticed that our two applet classes, `OldButtoner` and `Buttoner`, are nearly identical. The only significant difference is that one creates a `GraphicButton` object, and the other creates an `AnimatedButton`. Create a new applet, named `NewButtoner`, which consolidates these two applets into one. `NewButtoner`, like the original versions of its predecessors, should accept parameters for its image file pattern, the number of images, a label, and a destination URL. Based, though, on the value of the "numPix" parameter, NewButtoner should attempt to create a button of the appropriate type. If the value of numPix is greater than 2, an animated button should be produced; otherwise, a graphic button will be created. As before, it no numPix parameter is specified, or an illegal number is entered for its value, NewButtoner should simply create a default Java button.

2. Using your "locking buttons" version of GraphicButton, create an applet that produces a "locking button group"—that is, a collection of locking graphic buttons displayed in a single panel, only one of which can be "down" at any time.

3. Finally, add customized versions of your button applets (you supply the images, the labels, and the URLs) to an HTML document of your own devising.